AROUND
COVENTRY
IN OLD PHOTOGRAPHS

NEW STREET photographed at Easter in 1908. First mentioned in 1384, New Street was believed to have been built to house the workers who created St Michael's (off picture left). The street, which was full of ancient timbered buildings, was demolished partly by bombs and partly by developers after the Second World War. It ran practically in a straight line from St Michael's Avenue to Cox Street. The area is now covered by Coventry Polytechnic.

AROUND
COVENTRY
IN OLD PHOTOGRAPHS

COLLECTED BY
DAVID McGRORY

Budding
BOOKS

A Budding Book

First published in 1991 by Alan Sutton Publishing Limited

This edition published in 1998 by Budding Books,
an imprint of Sutton Publishing Limited
Phoenix Mill · Thrupp · Stroud · Gloucestershire GL5 2BU

A catalogue record for this book is available from the British Library

ISBN 1-84015-025-4

DEDICATION

For my Mum
Beryl McGrory
(1922–1987)

Typesetting and origination by
Sutton Publishing Limited.
Printed in Great Britain by
WBC Limited, Bridgend, Mid-Glamorgan.

CONTENTS

INTRODUCTION

Coventry lies in the centre of England; originally in the county of Warwickshire it was granted the status of county by King Henry VI in 1451. The city remained the City and County of Coventry until 1842 when it reverted back to Warwickshire. The city now lies in the politically created West Midlands and awaits its rightful return to its native county which surrounds it on nearly all sides.

The city's early history is obscure as very little evidence written or otherwise remains of the pre-twelfth-century settlement. Apart from the odd Roman coin and other related objects, plus a large Roman hoard found in Foleshill, there is no firm evidence of any Roman occupation in the area. Tradition states that a Roman general had a fortified camp erected on Barr's Hill and in the past Roman coins have come to light here. In all probability an ancient trackway must have existed here taking travellers towards the Fosse Way, past the camp at Baginton.

The origin of the city's name is equally as obscure as its early history. One personal theory is that somewhere along the ancient track which passed through here a shrine was erected next to a ford on the Sherbourne or by one of the three great pools which existed here. The shrine was dedicated to a minor Celtic-Roman water goddess called Coventina. Modern authorities tend to favour Cofantreo, first used in 1053 to mean Cofa's tree, the tree being the boundary mark of an early settler.

One of the earliest written references to Coventry is the reported sacking of St Osburg's nunnery (founded AD 700) by marauding Danes led by Edric the Traitor, in the year 1016. The nunnery may have stood between the Burges and Trinity Street.

Coventry's world-famous Lady Godiva and her husband, Earl Leofric, the fifth Earl of Mercia, founded a great Benedictine priory here in 1043, and dedicated it to St Mary the Virgin. An idea of the magnificence of the priory church can be gained from William of Malmesbury who wrote that, 'it was enriched and beautified with so much gold and silver that the walls seemed too narrow to contain it, insomuch that Robert de Limesie, bishop of this diocese in the time of King William Rufus, scraped from one beam that supported the shrines 500 marks of silver.'

Lady Godiva's (Godgifu) legendary naked ride through the market place, to relieve the citizens of Coventry from her husband's heavy taxation, is known throughout much of the modern world. Godiva herself was far too old at the time of the supposed event and it is most likely that the event is a memory of a local pagan fertility ritual.

A few years after Godiva's death a castle was built in the city by the Earls of Chester, its main entrance being Broadgate, the city's heart to this day. This castle often found itself under a state of seige. It is recorded that the great Earl Marmion of Tamworth laid seige to the castle and fortified the priory. His attempted seizure of the castle came to a sudden end when the earl died after his horse had thrown him violently into his own defensive ditches.

One piece of the city's history is recorded by Shakespeare himself in *Richard II*, Act I, Scene III. Shakespeare recalls an event which took place on Gosford Green in the year 1397, when Henry Bolingbroke, Duke of Hereford (later Henry IV) and Thomas Mowbray, Duke of Norfolk, met here on the green before the king and ten thousand fully armoured knights, to fight a duel of combat. Before the combat could begin the king rose from his throne and called a halt to the proceedings and banished both knights from the land.

Richard II was but one of many monarchs who came to Coventry, earning it the title of the 'resort of kings and queens'. This resort's most outstanding feature, apart from its churches, was its massive defensive wall, circling the city and containing thirty-two gates and towers. This nearly two-and-a-half-mile long, nine-foot thick wall was considered by many to be second only to the one which surrounded London.

Coventry is known as an industrial city, it is however fairly green compared with many northern industrial areas. Its industries date back to medieval times with the processing of wool and weaving, an art which would be practised in the city in various forms until the collapse of the silk-weaving industry in 1861. The watch-trade, which began in the city in the seventeenth century, expanded and other manufacturing industries emerged, such as the production of sewing machines, the bicycle, motorcycle and the motor car. As Coventry is the birthplace of the British motor car, and the city had a very large number of manufacturers, for the purposes of this book the industry is represented by the Daimler Company (now the Jaguar-Daimler), the country's first mass producer of the motor car.

The city's industrialization was the major factor which led to its growth and varied population. The process began in the late nineteenth century, and with the expanding industrialization came large population growth, a trend which continued into the 1960s. The boundary extensions of the city, taking in the outer villages, began in the 1890s when the districts such as Radford, Earlsdon, Foleshill and Stoke were taken into the city. In reality the city had hardly grown to any extent outside the area formed by the long-gone medieval city wall. The city had grown within itself by infilling, building in the grounds of larger older houses.

Up until before the Second World War the city still contained many ancient buildings. J.B. Priestly, one of many famous persons to visit the city wrote of his visit, 'I knew it was an old place, but I was surprised to find how much of the past, in soaring stone and carved wood, still remained in the city.'

Much destruction was wrought upon the old city from the beginning of the twentieth century in the guise of redevelopment and slum clearance. Destruction of a different kind came on the night of 14 November 1940, when the German Luftwaffe, prompted by the city's industrialization, rained tons of high explosives and thousands of incendiary bombs on the city, setting its heart ablaze. Great was the courage of the people of Coventry on that long night of death and destruction.

The city became the first in history to suffer saturation bombing and a new word for destruction was coined, 'Coventrated'.

After the war's devastation peace returned and so did the need to rebuild. The remains of the old city centre were unceremoniously wiped clear for the planners to create a new type of city centre. A carefully laid out pedestrian shopping centre was created in what became known as 'Festival of Britain' style. The second major project in the city was to rebuild St Michael's. The new cathedral attached to the old is a treasure house of modernism and contains the largest tapestry in the world.

The zest for redevelopment before and after the war did as much, if not more, damage to the old city than many realized. After the last war there were over three hundred and fifty timber-framed buildings still standing in the city. By 1966 the number had been reduced to thirty-four pre-1700 buildings remaining. Old buildings still continue to be demolished, although most of these now tend to be Victorian.

This book is a testimony to the City of Coventry which hopefully will make the reader understand what the city was, what it became and why. Within the following pages can be found a lost city and some survivals which remind us of Coventry's proud historic past.

The majority of photographs in the following pages are reproduced from the Coventry and Warwickshire Collection housed within the local studies section of Coventry's Central Library.

Broadgate:
The City's Heart

BROADGATE in the 1920s. The heart of Coventry.

A RARE PHOTOGRAPH OF BROADGATE taken in the 1860s by Coventry chemist, Joseph Wingrave, whose premises stood on the corner of High Street and Pepper Lane. The Brodeyate, as it was known, was first mentioned in the twelfth century and formed the main entrance to Coventry Castle which stood near this place. Here, between the Norman castle and the long-gone priory of St Mary, died the great Earl Marmion of Tamworth, who fell into one of his own defensive ditches while placing the castle under a state of seige. Many major events took place in ancient Broadgate. Here kings and queens have walked in stately array. Justice too was meted out here, barbaric executions of attemped regicides and more lordly individuals whose heads and limbs were used to adorn the city gates. Broadgate was widened in 1820 and most of its medieval buildings were demolished. During later demolition work in 1929 the building at the top of the photograph with white window surrounds, then the Coventry Arms, was found to have not only large decorated medieval fireplaces, but also spacious medieval vaulted cellars. The National Bank, now the National Westminster, was built on the site. Broadgate in the late nineteenth century was fondly called the 'Top of the Town' and was then, as now, a meeting place for the citizens of Coventry.

LOOKING DOWN BROADGATE into Cross Cheaping on market day in 1863. The decorative archway of greenery and flags were erected in celebration of the marriage of Prince Edward (later Edward VII) to the Danish Princess Alexandra. Like the previous photograph this shows Broadgate on market day shortly before the introduction of a by-law which moved all the street markets into a newly developed and enlarged market square on the site of the old Butter or Women's Market.

THE JUNCTION OF BROADGATE AND CROSS CHEAPING in the 1860s. In the centre of the photograph is Waterloo House, which in its earlier form was known as the Mayor's Parlour. Here the city mayors resided, such as Alderman John Hewitt, three times mayor of Coventry and Warwickshire's greatest eighteenth-century 'thief-taker'. The archway led into Market Place and on into Market Square, both destroyed during the Second World War. If Waterloo House still existed today it would probably stand near Owen Owen and the Hotel Leofric.

A FINE JOSEPH WINGRAVE PHOTOGRAPH taken around 1860. This is the Women's or Butter Market, built in 1719 in the yard of the Peacock Inn, next to the Watch-house and stocks. It was here that the father of Methodism, John Wesley, preached on his first visit to the city after being refused permission to use St Mary's Hall, the mayor giving preference to a dancing master. The building behind the market house on the left had a small room in it in which the followers of Wesley used to worship. John Wesley wrote in his journal that, 'the poor little flock at Coventry have at length procured a neat convenient room, only it is far too small.' The size of this room led to Wesley preaching under the shelter of this market house late on a wet morning in the year 1779. The market house and adjoining buildings were demolished in 1865 to make way for a new market square and hall. The entire site now lies under the present Hotel Leofric.

THIS SHOP IN MARKET PLACE awaits demolition as the area prepares to be cleared for the building of the new market square and hall which was opened in 1867. Mary Ann Laxon & Sons, Cheese and Bacon Factors, moved from these somewhat grubby sixteenth-century premises to the new market hall in about 1868. Their shop and factory facing down Market Street late became the Fish Market.

THE MARKET HALL AND CLOCK opened on 2 December 1867. The 100-ft high clock tower soon became a city landmark, well remembered by old Coventrians. The clock itself was installed in 1870 and was considered one of the most accurate in the country. Its creator, Edward Thomas Loseby, was so confident in his own skill that he signed a contract to the effect that he would pay £1 for every second the clock lost. Suffice it to say Loseby never needed to honour the agreement. On 14 November 1940, when bombs rained down upon the city, all around the clock tower was flattened and the clock ticked on. Eventually the tower was demolished as it was supposed to be unsafe and the clock mechanism was removed. When the puppet clock was installed in Broadgate and its electric motor failed, Loseby's mechanism was installed and it works the clock up to the present day.

A BUSTLING SCENE IN MARKET SQUARE (known to many as West Orchard Market) in 1910. The square which changed little until its destruction in 1940 also functioned as a meeting place. Here, many a politician aired his views on a Sunday evening to a packed audience. On the left can be seen the Market Hall, then the Fish Market. The street in the background is West Orchard which started in Cross Cheaping and ended at the bottom of Smithford Street, now under the Lower Precinct. The pub on the right was later known as the Market Tavern and nicknamed the Hole in the Wall, due to a large cartoon which hung on the wall behind the bar. After the war the bombed market site continued to be used as a makeshift market, until 1953 when it was moved to derelict land in Corporation Street where the ill-fated Rex Cinema stood.

THE JUNCTION OF BROADGATE, High Street, Hertford Street and Smithford Street. Peeping Tom stares down from his corner window as a hackney carriage awaits a fare on a quiet summer's morning in 1863. The original King's Head is just around the corner.

THE SAME JUNCTION in 1931. Peeping Tom is now in the enlarged King's Head Hotel and on the left can be seen the only surviving recognizable feature left in Broadgate today: the National Westminster Bank.

The Cross, Coventry. W5890.

BROADGATE in 1898. This fine view looking down Broadgate into Cross Cheaping was often called the Cross, for it was the site of the Coventry Cross, a smaller copy of which now stands at the back of Holy Trinity church. On the right stands the Royal Wine and Spirit Vaults, the landlord of that time being one William Flane. Next to the Vaults was a narrow lane which led into Butcher Row and onward to Holy Trinity church. The tram at this time was in its early stages and the hackney carriage still picked up fares in the centre of Broadgate. The prominent ladder had no connection with the newly erected (1895) electric tram lines, but was in fact a fire ladder serving the surrounding buildings.

BROADGATE looking north into Cross Cheaping in 1931. The shops here remembered by most are Burtons (still trading), Astleys (a trader in the city for over two hundred years), H. Samuel (still trading), David Burdetts, bookseller and stationer (no longer trading), Millets (stopped trading recently), Hiltons, Whitfields, J. Lyons & Co. and Kendalls.

TWO TRAMS, INCLUDING THE NO. SIX, TO BROAD LANE. This photograph, taken in the 1930s, shows the National Provincial Bank (now the National Westminster) in the background. To the right of the trams Hertford Street can be seen. Most of this area now lies under the new Cathedral Lanes shopping centre.

A DETAIL OF THE JUNCTION OF BROADGATE and Cross Cheaping taken in 1935. Behind the tram terminal can be seen the Vaults and Hiltons Boots & Shoes which stood on either side of the alley to Butcher Row. This photograph was taken as the buildings awaited demolition to make way for Trinity Street.

CROSS CHEAPING awaiting demolition in 1935. A continuation of the above photograph, this detailed view shows the cobbled entrance (left) to the old Market Hall and Square, the site of which now lies under the Hotel Leofric.

BROADGATE just before its total destruction on the night of 14 November 1940. Note the sandbags and that the windows of the shop on the right are taped up against bomb blast. The photograph was taken from the recently erected Owen Owen store, the predecessor of the present larger building. On the left is Trinity Street and on the right Cross Cheaping. The sole survivor of the night of destruction was the bank (top centre).

THREE COVENTRY TRAMS in 1941, with nowhere to go. The photograph shows Nos 63, 64 and 65 at Foleshill tram depot which stood on the corner of Foleshill Road and Lythalls Lane. The trams were waiting to be scrapped as the city's tram-line system had been rendered unusable after the bombing on 14 November 1940. This ended the use of the tram in Coventry, which had started life as early as 1884 with the introduction of the steam tram. The electric tram system came into use in 1895 and soon became an everyday sight associated with Broadgate, whose fate it shared.

SECTION TWO

From Spon End to Gosford Green

LOOKING DOWN SMITHFORD STREET around 1900.

SPON END around 1906. These buildings stood beyond Spon Bridge and some have sandstone bases which were probably pillaged from the old city gate, Spon Gate, which was demolished in 1771.

THIS RATHER DICKENSIAN VIEW was taken from Spon Bridge in Spon Street on 1 March 1914. The River Sherbourne still flows openly here, but as it winds through the city centre it now disappears underground, running through huge pipes. Looking at this scene back in 1914 and today, it is hard to believe that once the owners of all such buildings that butted on to the Sherbourne had rights to fish the water. Fish included pike, perch and trout.

THE CHAPEL OF ST JAMES AND ST CHRISTOPHER in Spon Street around 1910. This fourteenth-century wayfarers' chapel next to Spon Bridge had a long and varied history as a religious house, then a private dwelling, always occupied until 1936. Before the Second World War the building was as it appears in the photograph, and plans were being made to preserve it. The war brought these plans to a halt and the building suffered some minor bomb damage, and eventually the building began to deteriorate. In the 1950s the council decided that it would be cheaper to turn the building into a ruin and this ruin now stands amid concrete tower blocks.

LOOKING UP SPON STREET around 1910. This photograph shows workers leaving the Rudge – Whitworth works, which employed over 1,800 people and was in its time the largest bicycle factory in the world. The works, now the former GEC and the first steel-framed factory building in the country, is presently under demolition.

BONDS HOSPITAL between Spon and Hill Street in 1910. The building was founded in 1506 by Thomas Bond, a Coventry draper, to house poor aged men. This it has done ever since and within recent years extended its intake by adding sheltered flats behind this beautiful structure.

SHARING THE SAME COURTYARD with the above is Bablake School. It was founded by Thomas Wheatley in 1560 because of a fortunate mistake. It is said that Wheatley, who was later mayor, sent for a shipment of steel ingots from Spain, and instead of steel ingots he received a chest of silver ingots, and as the source could not be traced he used this unexpected wealth to set up Bablake School. Here boys were educated and later placed as apprentices with respectable trades. The building is now used as offices.

THE CHURCH OF ST JOHN THE BAPTIST in Fleet Street first became a parish church in 1734. It was founded by Queen Isabella in May 1344 as a collegiate chapel in which priests would pray for the soul of her dead husband, King Edward II. The church stopped being used for worship after the Dissolution (1590s). It then served as a place of internment for Scottish rebels captured after the Battle of Preston during the Civil War in 1648. Those rebels who served the king were shunned, or 'Sent to Coventry', by the people of Parliamentarian-held Coventry. Later the church was used as stables, a market and then a winding and dying house for cloth. The photograph probably dates from before 1861 when much of the external stonework was replaced. The building on the far left is what remains of the old city bridewell, a place of confinement for petty offenders which fell from use in 1831. This remnant of a long narrow building dating from 1571 was used as a malthouse until around 1861. Inmates would hang brightly coloured knitted purses from the small high windows in the hope the people passing through the narrow thoroughfare below would spare a penny or two.

FLEET STREET between Smithford and Hill Street in 1929. On the left can be seen St John's and on the right the shops include the Oriental Café and the Coventry & District Dairy Co. The buildings were to be demolished for the laying of Corporation Street.

SMITHFORD STREET as it appeared in 1905. This view was taken from the corner of Hertford Street. In the distance can be seen the tower of St John's church.

LOOKING DOWN SMITHFORD STREET from Broadgate in the 1860s. This street, which was one of the city's main thoroughfares, got its name from the fact that its lower end, now under the Co-op in the Lower Precinct, crossed the River Sherbourne here at the Smiths-ford, later bridged by Rams Bridge. The course of the road since the city centre was rebuilt, now follows from the High Street, though the shops under Broadgate House, onwards through the middle of the Precinct by Marks & Spencer and down through the Co-op and finally coming out by St John's church. In the above Wingrave photograph the top-hatted policeman, or Peeler as he was known, is actually standing at the top of Broadgate. To his right is the Coventry Hotel and to his left Peeping Tom can be seen looking down from his window on the corner of Hertford Street. If the policeman stood in the same place now and looked up he would see the Godiva puppet clock.

A CONTINUATION OF THE LAST VIEW, this extraordinary photograph taken from the High Street looking down Smithford Street was photographed from outside Wingrave's shop; the angle suggests that he must have set his camera up on the roof of a carriage. In this 1860s view, on the left next to Greyfriars Lane can be seen the offices of the *Coventry Standard*, a forerunner of the *Coventry Evening Telegraph*. The cobbled area on the right is Broadgate and the first building on the right in the High Street took a direct hit during the November blitz.

THE HIGH STREET was first mentioned in the thirteenth century as a continuation of Earl Street. In this Wingrave view of the 1860s can be seen (on the left) Atkins & Turton Tea & Coffee Merchants who traded in the city, I believe, up until the 1950s. Atkins & Turton later became Martin's Bank, then later a branch of the Coventry Economic Building Society. The building was demolished during the redevelopment of Broadgate in 1990. The next building across the narrow Pepper Lane is the photographer's own chemist shop, dating back to the sixteenth century. Deeds existed for the next building down which dated it to the year 1587, built in the twenty-ninth year of the reign of Elizabeth I. Both these ancient buildings were restored in the mid-1930s only to be destroyed during the 14 November 1940 raid.

THE CRAVEN ARMS, High Street was originally an Elizabethan inn called the White Bear. It was partially rebuilt in 1802 and completely rebuilt in 1914. The landlord of the inn for forty years was white-whiskered Dan Claridge, considered to be one of the finest coachmen in the country. Dan, a staunch believer in the coach, tried, on more than one occasion, to revive the public's interest in this disappearing means of transport. The photograph shows one of Dan's revivals when he ran a coach service between Coventry and Birmingham from June to September in the year 1899, two years after the birth of the motor car. The last regular coach to run between Coventry and London was driven by Dan on Wednesday, 12 August 1874. When Dan was interviewed by a local newspaper in the 1890s he said Coventry was full of foreigners and not at all like it was in the 'good old days' when everyone waved and shouted 'Good morning Mr Claridge'. Dan's dream of the rebirth of the coaching age died with the birth of the motor car in Sandy Lane, Radford. Dan Claridge died in April 1923 after a number of years at the other Craven Arms in Binley. The High Street Craven Arms site is now occupied by Barclays Bank.

THE REAR OF THE CRAVEN ARMS in the 1860s. This is part of a large stable block which served the inn, holding up to forty horses. The stables and most of the original inn survived until their demolition late in 1913. Ironically the building which replaced the original Tudor one was 'mock Tudor'.

THE NEWLY-WIDENED HIGH STREET in 1928. Mid-left can be seen the rebuilt Craven Arms, now a re-fronted branch of Barclays Bank. To its right is Waters of Coventry, wine merchants, who are now to leave the city after trading here since 1802. The building jutting out is the Coventry Arms which stood at the top of Broadgate. Known locally as the Swinging Arms, because of its Wild West-style doors, the pub was demolished during the tenancy of Walter 'Dolly' Newman in November 1928.

BUILDING THE COUNCIL HOUSE in 1916. The City Council House in Earl Street was constructed between 1913 and 1917, being delayed by the outbreak of the First World War. The competition-winning building was designed to be in keeping with St Mary's Hall at the rear. The Birmingham architect's design got a mixed reception from the people of Coventry as it spoiled the view of the spires. Despite being in use since 1917, the Duke of York (later George VI) did not officially open it until 1920. The red-sandstone building was decorated with various sculptures and carvings. This was, in September 1925, added to with Portland stone figures over the main entrance of historical people associated with the city, such as Lady Godiva and Earl Leofric. During the blitz, despite having every window blown out, the building remained relatively undamaged. After his surprise visit to see the damage to the city on 16 November 1940, King George VI ate a cold meal by candle-light here.

THIS PHOTOGRAPH WAS TAKEN on Sunday, 24 May 1914 and shows the setting off of an old-fashioned stage-coach from the George Inn in Little Park Street to Stratford. The coach called *The Olden Times* was formerly the Coventry to London coach which was owned and driven by Dan Claridge, landlord of the Craven Arms. The driver of the coach on this particular trip into nostalgia was Thomas Henley (in top hat), a well-known Midland teamster. The coach and four went via Kenilworth, Warwick, Barford, Charlecote and Leddington, reaching Stratford in three hours. The group then had lunch at the Black Swan, followed by a trip along the river, with running commentary by Arthur Lole, landlord of the George Inn. This was the first of many such runs to Shakespeare's birthplace. The site of the George Inn is now by Little Park Street police headquarters.

THE PALACE YARD, once known as the Crown House, photographed in the 1860s. Palace Yard stood opposite the Council House in Earl Street directly across from the building's last bay next to the tower on the junction with St Mary's lane. The fifteenth-century mansion built around a central courtyard belonged to the Hopkins family for over two hundred years. It was here that Princess Elizabeth (daughter of James I, and later Queen of Bohemia) was brought for safety out of reach of the Catholic conspirators who had tried to blow up king and parliament on 5 November 1605. If all went to plan Prince Henry or Elizabeth was to have become a puppet monarch in a Catholic-controlled England. Here also stayed the ill-fated James II on his visit to the city in 1687, a year before he fled the country. When the Palace Yard left the hands of the Hopkins family, it became many things including a school, a coaching inn, builders yard (as above), printing office, ribbon warehouse and finally craft shops, before the Second World War. Up until the 1930s the massive oak doors to the main courtyard bore the names of different coaches painted upon the panels from its days as an inn. This fine building, well loved and remembered by many, was completely destroyed by a direct hit during the 14 November raid.

STONE ARBOUR standing in the grounds of Little Palace Yard (demolished 1961) in Little Park Street. This sandstone arbour, despite bearing the date 1701, is thought to have dated from the fifteenth or sixteenth century. It, together with sections of garden wall joining with the Palace Yard, were decorated with carvings of exotic animals, such as rhino, elephant, bear, tiger etc. When the property was purchased by Bushill & Sons Ltd, builders, in 1930, the arbour was presented to the city. It was removed and re-erected in the War Memorial Park in April 1930. Amazingly, despite being well outside the city centre, the arbour took a direct hit from a stray bomb during the blitz and was literally blown to pieces.

WHITEFRIARS GATE in Much Park Street. This gateway, built in 1352, formed the outer gateway to Whitefriars monastery which lies some several hundred yards away. Through this gateway once passed all the traffic from the London Road. Charles Dickens passed through here and referred to the gate in his novel, *The Old Curiosity Shop*. The gateway is now a toy museum.

JORDAN WELL STREET got its name early in the fifteenth century from a large communal well which served the area. The road runs between the junctions of Bayley Lane and Cox Street. The view, taken around 1908, shows Jordan Well to have had many timbered buildings. Despite the blitz some survived below the Herbert Art Gallery and Museum; these however were demolished in the early 1960s.

A VIEW OF GOSFORD STREET, taken in the 1860s. This is the left-hand side of the street at the bottom of the hill, past the present labour exchange. Gosford Street was first mentioned in the twelfth century, and here in the centre of the road stood the medieval Swines Cross, a market cross by which cattle were brought to be sold. Beyond this point the road narrowed as it approached Gosford Gate (demolished 1765). King Edward IV was refused permission to enter the city through this gate and later in 1605 Princess Elizabeth was brought through the gate from Coombe Abbey to the safety of the walled city. Next to Gosford Gate on the bridge over the Sherbourne stood St George's chapel, dedicated to England's patron saint, claimed by local legend to be Coventry-born.

THIS PHOTOGRAPH, taken in 1927, shows the never-ending destruction of Coventry's ancient timbered buildings. The buildings in the background stood on the corner of Gosford and Lower Ford Street. The street still has some remaining timbered buildings; their age hidden beneath bricks, plaster and paintwork.

THE CORNER OF FAR GOSFORD STREET AND PAYNES LANE, about 1925. This scene has changed recently with the building of the Sky Blue Way relief road. The buildings top left were demolished and the traffic mainly diverted, much to the discontent of the street's traders. The railings on the left mark the corner of Gosford Green, the site of the intended combat between the Dukes of Norfolk and Hereford, and the spot where Earl Rivers and his son were beheaded in 1469.

WHITEFRIARS MONASTERY, next to the London Road, taken in the 1880s. The present monastic house of Whitefriars is but a small reminder of a much larger monastic estate which contained numerous buildings and a spired church. The estate was founded in 1342 by Sir John Poultney of London, a wealthy draper of Warwickshire descent. After the Dissolution in 1536 the estate was granted to John Hales who demolished most of the buildings and church and turned the main cloister into a private house. Here he entertained Queen Elizabeth I who during her visit is said to have spoken to the people of Coventry from the oriel window seen in the photograph. During the Civil War in the 1640s when Charles I and his army tried to breach nearby New Gate, Lady Hales and a serving woman were killed as cannon fire struck the building. In 1801 the building was purchased by a combined church poor relief group and converted into a workhouse, probably the first in England. It remained a workhouse until its closure in 1943, then it was used as a refuge for down-and-outs. It is now a tourist attraction and art gallery, and despite being next to the city's noisy ring-road, Whitefriars stills retains a silent peace within its walls.

WHITEFRIARS CLOISTERS, used as the workhouse dining room, in 1928.

THE CHARTERHOUSE off the London Road in 1952. This building began life as part of a much larger Carthusian grange founded in 1381. Like nearby Whitefriars it fell from use after the Dissolution and its surrounding buildings were destroyed. The Charterhouse remained in private hands for about four hundred years until Col. Sir William Wyley, ex-city mayor, the building's last private occupant, presented it to the city in 1940.

Greyfriars Green to Bishop Street

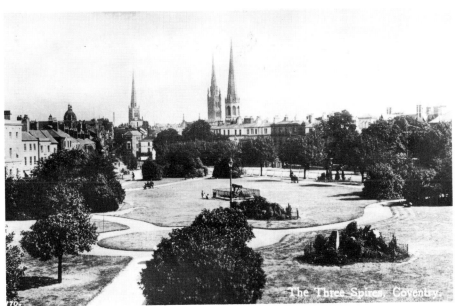

GREYFRIARS GREEN and the three spires in around 1912.

Coventry from the Green. W6434

GREYFRIARS GREEN and Coventry's famous spires in 1898. Once known as Cheylesmore Green, the area began life as waste land on which the city freemen held rights to graze cattle. The green was often used in the late eighteenth century by the various cavalry regiments stationed in the nearby barracks. Up until 1858 the green was the site of Coventry Fair before it was moved to Pool Meadow. In 1875 the area lost its grazing rights and the city council decided to improve it and turn it into a public space. The statue of Sir Thomas White, a London merchant and city benefactor, was erected in 1882 on the site of the old Horse Pool, nicknamed the 'Red Sea', for when wagoners and coachmen drove their vehicles into the pool to water the horses, wash the vehicles or tighten the wheels, the water turned a rich red due to the local clay which lined the pool. Despite changes to the green this area remains basically unchanged to this day.

JUST BELOW THE GREEN, looking up Hertford Street and Warwick Lane. Before Hertford Street was opened in 1813, all traffic from this direction entered the city through Greyfriars Gate (dismantled October 1781) up Warwick Lane and into Greyfriars Lane. On the right is Christchurch, the smallest and oldest of the city spires. The body of the church in the photograph was erected in 1830/2 and attached to the tower and spire of the original early fourteenth-century church, built by the Greyfriars or Franciscans as part of their friary. The original church, despite much opposition, was demolished after the Dissolution leaving only the tower standing, in what later became an orchard. At one point in time the owner of the ruin used it as a pigsty; it quickly became known as the tallest pigsty in England! Next to the church is the Temperance Hotel, now the site of the central Methodist Hall. This was originally the churchyard in which were buried such notables as Thomas Harrington, who was beheaded for claiming to be the Duke of Clarence. Also, Sir Henry Mumford and Sir Robert Mallorie were laid to rest here minus their heads, which decorated the city gates. In the top window on the left is a representation of Peeping Tom. This effigy can now be found above the covered way at the top of Hertford Street.

CHRISTCHURCH in the 1920s. The second body of the church was destroyed by bombs in April 1941. The tower which once again stands alone has now been converted into a shop selling Italian pottery.

THE JUNCTION OF HERTFORD STREET AND WARWICK LANE. This photograph taken around 1931 shows the timbered Grapes Inn and below it the old Methodist Hall. All await demolition for the rebuilding of the present Methodist Central Hall.

LOOKING UP HERTFORD STREET in 1930. From the bottom right is George Loveitt, W.H. Smith, -?-, -?-, the Queen's Head Hotel, Coventry Savings Bank, central post office and the National (now National Westminster) Bank.

THE SAME VIEW taken in the early 1940s. The rubble from the bombed and burnt-out buildings below the post office has been cleared and some normality returns to Hertford Street. This part of the street is now a covered walkway and W.H. Smith has left the street (April 1991) and re-opened in the new West Orchard shopping centre.

THE KING'S HEAD HOTEL on the corner of Hertford Street and Smithford Street. The age of the original building is unknown, but is likely to be medieval. In the eighteenth century the original inn which stood around the corner in Smithford Street was a favourite billet of commissioned officers. When the old inn was demolished in the late 1870s, much of its fine Chippendale and Sheridan furniture came under the hammer. The new King's Head extended round the corner into Hertford Street using much of the land at the rear which belonged to the original inn. Part of the building built by Mr George Woodcock opened its doors by Christmas 1879; it was however some time before the whole luxurious building was completed. Many remember its fine corner tap room decorated with stained glass depicting scenes from the city past. The King's Head was completely destroyed on the night of 14 November 1940. The building jutting out is the City Hotel, on the corner of Smithford Street and Broadgate. The buildings in the distance are the top of Cross Cheaping. Note the fancy wrought-iron balcony and beautiful street lamps in this 1892 photograph.

THE KING'S HEAD from Broadgate. The top corner window was the home of the Peeping Tom figure now in Cathedral Lanes from 1870 to 1939. This view was taken in 1900.

THE KING'S HEAD. In the foreground of this photograph, taken in 1929, workmen prepare the foundations for the new National Provincial Bank, now the National Westminster. A landmark in Broadgate since its erection and Broadgate's only surviving pre-war building.

CROSS CHEAPING in 1906. This top part of Cross Cheaping below Broadgate down to the Dresden's Tailors sign now lies under Owen Owen. Just past the Dresden sign is West Orchard leading to the market and onwards to the bottom of Smithford Street.

THE SAME VIEW A LITTLE FURTHER DOWN, taken in the late 1930s. Below the changing façades on the left the street remained unchanged. On the right, however, the street had been demolished for the building of the first Owen Owen department store, which would shortly be destroyed itself in November 1940. The opening on the left is West Orchard.

CROSS CHEAPING AND THE BURGES. This early photograph, taken in the 1860s, shows the sixteenth-century building, on the left, seen in the previous photograph on the corner of West Orchard. Like the previous photographs, nothing here still exists. There are, however, some eighteenth-century buildings surviving on the right-hand side of the Burges. Bus ranks now line the left-hand side of this street which was once known as St John's Bridges because of the two bridges here which carried people over the River Sherbourne. The building jutting out at the bottom of the street marks the corner of Well and Bishop Street.

Old Grammar School, Coventry

THE OLD GRAMMAR SCHOOL on the corner of Hales and Bishop Street in 1908. This fourteenth-century building was originally the church of the Hospital of St John. The hospital, itself now gone, was built in the twelfth century to provide refuge for the poor and sick, also wayfarers in need. The building which now stands was given in the sixteenth century to John Hales of Whitefriars who converted it into a grammar school, which it remained until 1885. Later it became a mission room and is now sadly in a bad way, and used only for jumble sales. The building originally extended across Hales Street, but was demolished when the road was constructed in the 1830s.

TIMBERED HOUSES IN WELL STREET in 1898, a once-familiar sight in old Coventry, near the corner at the bottom of Bishop Street. The street was named after a large draw well which served it, under the rear of the present Equity and Law building. Here in this street James Starley created the differential gear which would revolutionize world transport.

TENANTS EJECTED FROM CONDEMNED PROPERTY in Well Street around 1912/13. Sadly a familiar sight in a city which was forever changing. It is interesting to note that most of this family's furniture dates from the 1860s.

OUT OF WELL STREET and back into the bottom right-hand side of Bishop Street. The building jutting out is referred to on p. 51 and lay on the corner of Well Street. It and other adjoining buildings were demolished for the construction of Corporation Street, opened in 1931. Most of the other buildings are now gone except for a small group which includes the present Parsons Nose chip shop which is next to the lamp-post.

A MAGNIFICENT VIEW FROM THE TOP OF BISHOP STREET, taken in 1875. Once on this spot stood Bishop Gate (demolished 1764) covering the road which forked to Radford and Foleshill. It was through this gate that Queen Elizabeth I and her huge retinue entered the city for her visit in 1565. Halfway down the street at the junction of Silver Street stood the medieval Swines Cross (taken down 1763), which marked the site of the pig, horse and cattle market which took place here well into the nineteenth century. Bishop Street was the main northern entrance to the city until the ring-road was constructed in the 1960s. This view minus one or two buildings with the spires of St Michael (left) and Holy Trinity (right) was a familiar view to Coventrians who entered the city from the north for centuries. On the right and left can be seen the Castle Inn (demolished in the 1960s) and the Cranes Inn, both of early eighteenth-century origin, and both involved with the story of the 'Coventry Gang' who were hanged on Whitley Common on 10 August 1763.

SECTION FOUR

Lady Godiva and Peeping Tom

THE FESTIVAL OF BRITAIN GODIVA PROCESSION in 1951. Ann Wrigg, a university student and actress, plays the part of Lady Godiva.

THE STORY OF HOW LADY GODIVA rode naked through the market place to free the people of Coventry from her husband's heavy taxation is known the world over. In all probability the ride never happened and probably has its origins in an early pagan fertility ritual. Despite this

the legend of Godiva continues and this photograph taken in Broadgate in 1907 proves the drawing power of the legendary lady. Here Godiva is represented by Patsy Montagu, an actress who went under the stage name of 'La Milo'.

A RARE PHOTOGRAPH of 1907 showing Godiva leaving St Mary's Hall. This was the traditional starting place for the procession since its conception in 1678. Within the hall's courtyard was a stone known as 'Lady Godiva's Mounting Block', which assisted the various Godivas to mount their white steeds.

THE PROCESSION of 1911 was scheduled to coincide with the coronation of King George V. Lady Godiva was represented by the extremely popular Miss Viola Hamilton, an actress from Hendon. Here she is seen in Far Gosford Street leading a procession which consisted of 250 people in costume and thousands of school children. The nun seen leading the lady's horse appears for the first time, due to the popularity of a print on sale which shows such a scene painted by Jules Lefebvre in 1899.

THE GODIVA PEACE PROCESSION of 1919 to mark the end of the Great War ended with a bang; literally. Godiva was played by actress Gladys Mann, who had left the city only four years earlier and moved to Dublin. Despite looking stunning in her Saxon countess dress, she caused great surprise and annoyance to many Coventrians for breaking the tradition of the lady riding in an undressed state. The day began with Lady Godiva leading the procession from Pool Meadow, which contained some twenty thousand children. The day successfully ended with firework displays around the city's parks. This was followed unexpectedly by the outbreak of riots in Broadgate which would continue for two more nights. See top photograph on p. 106.

Frances P. Burchell

GODIVA RODE ON, while the storm clouds gathered over Europe. In 1936, Miss Frances Burchell, aged twenty-two, of Harbourne, Birmingham, was the winner of a 'find this year's Godiva' competition. She beat over sixty candidates who wished to play Coventry's famed benefactress and by all accounts played her part well.

PEEPING TOM LOOKS DOWN upon Lady Godiva from his fourth-storey window in the King's Head Hotel. No one knows the origins of this enigmatic figure who was first recorded in 1659. Legend states that Tom was a tailor who peeped at Lady Godiva riding naked through the market place, and for his voyeurism he was struck blind. The oldest figure used to represent Peeping Tom is illustrated on these pages. It dates from around the early 1400s and is believed to be an oak figure of St George, who, as local legend states, was born and died in Coventry. The figure is thought to have been removed from either St George's Chapel which once stood in Gosford Street, or St Mary's Priory during their destruction after the Dissolution in the 1530s. The figure was first mentioned as representing Tom in 1659 looking from a window by the Coventry Cross, at the junction of Broadgate and Cross Cheaping (under the present Owen Owen). In 1678 Alderman Owen had it placed in an upper storey window of a house at the bottom of Greyfriars Lane. When the house was demolished around 1775, Thomas Sharp, hatter and noted local historian, obtained the figure and had it placed in a specially constructed window above his shop door near the corner of Smithford and Hertford Street. When Hertford Street was constructed in 1812/13, Sharp's shop became the corner house and the figure was placed in a specially constructed corner window, where he looked down into Hertford Street. In the late 1870s the King's Head was demolished and rebuilt on a larger scale, taking in the corner property. By Christmas 1879 Tom was back, now looking out of a fourth-storey window in the new hotel. Here he remained until the outbreak of war and the threat of possible air-raids prompted his removal to a safer place. On 14 November 1940 the hotel was completely destroyed by bombs. After this lucky escape the figure disappeared for a number of years until it finally reappeared minus its colourful paintwork in time to be placed in a glass case in the newly constructed Hotel Leofric. Tom was moved in March 1991 to the new Cathedral Lanes shopping centre. He now stands in a sealed glass case overlooking the bronze figure of Lady Godiva in Broadgate. There were three other Peeping Toms around the city, two of which were head and shoulder copies of the original Tom.

A DETAILED PHOTOGRAPH OF PEEPING TOM, taken in the courtyard of the old King's Head in the 1860s. The seven-foot high painted figure was decorated during Godiva processions with a cockade hat, medals and ribbons. Its arms were probably removed in the seventeenth century, so it could fit in its window.

COVENTRY ALSO HAD ITS CARNIVALS. This one in 1927 raised £27,000 for the Coventry and Warwickshire Hospital. The group on horseback are: Mrs I. Brooks as an Eastern princess; Mr T. Corfield, a bullfighter; Mr Alfred Smith, gladiator; Mrs Edith Smith, Indian squaw; and Mr L. Athersuch as the son of a sheik.

COVENTRY CARNIVAL QUEEN of 1928 coming from Smithford Street into Broadgate in her rather impressive swan chariot. The queen was Marjorie Biddulph and her maids of honour were Madge Collingbourne, Edith Varley, Lucy Page and Lucy Swain.

THE GODIVA PROCESSION of 1929 passing by Dunn's Corner, as this lower section of the King's Head Hotel came to be known. In front, as was the norm in past parades, can be seen St George. The individuals in the coach represent King George IV (visited 1807 and 1815); the Marquis of Hertford (from whom Hertford Street got its name); Lord Craven of Coombe Abbey; and Lord Nelson and Lady Hamilton who stayed at the King's Head during a surprise visit to the city in September 1802.

A LIVING REPRESENTATION OF THE CITY ARMS in the same procession in the lower end of the Burges. On the baby elephant's back is the golden castle surmounted by the cat'a'mountain, the emblem from the war helmet of the heroic Black Prince, son of Edward III who owned the manor of Cheylesmore. On the cloth can be seen the city motto, *camera principis*, the 'prince's chamber'.

The Cathedral Quarter

BAYLEY LANE in 1898. Unchanged to this day.

HOLY TRINITY CHURCH before its restoration in the 1860s. The first church on this site was built by the monks of nearby St Mary's Priory some time after 1043. The present building dates from the early thirteenth century and the late fifteenth century. This is with the exception of the spire which was erected in 1667, replacing the previous one which collapsed during a gale in 1665, killing a boy who was passing at the time. The exterior was originaly all red sandstone, however much has been replaced during various restorations with the lighter coloured ashlar grey sandstone. Famous individuals associated with the church are Doctor Philemon Holland, translator of many of the more notable Greek works; his memorial may be seen to the left of the entrance. Here England's greatest eighteenth-century actress Sarah Siddons (née Kemble) was married. The marriage, which took place on 24 November 1773, was frowned upon by Sarah's father who had forbidden her to marry an actor. When Roger Kemble accused his daughter of disobeying him and getting engaged to the worst actor in his company his daughter replied, 'Exactly father, nobody can call him an actor.' Another lady who was a more regular visitor to the church was Mary Ann Evans, better known to the world as the novelist George Eliot. She attended the church with her father who occasionally acted as plate-bearer. The church still exists today because of the vigilence of Canon Graham Clitheroe and his team of fire-watchers who fought and saved this ancient building as all around burnt on 14 November 1940. On the left can be seen the bell campanile which was erected in 1855 and nearly collapsed the following year when rung too vigorously to celebrate the end of the Crimean War. The campanile stood until the 1960s.

THE CHANCEL OF HOLY TRINITY in 1921. Above, out of the photograph, is a rare medieval Domesday painting and painted medieval roof. The fine fifteenth-century pulpit on the right is said to be one of the highest in the country. The fifteenth-century brass eagle lectern below the pulpit survived destruction during Cromwell's Commonwealth by being converted into a collection box. Money was placed in the eagle's beak and it was emptied at the tail.

THE CHURCH OF ST NICHOLAS, Radford was built in 1873 as a sister church to Holy Trinity. It was built from red sandstone quarried from the grounds of nearby Westfield House (demolished in 1990). Within this graveyard lay the remains of the Revd John George Wood, the father of Victorian popular natural history. Also Andrew Ernest 'Stoddy' Stoddart, fearless rugby player and victorious captain of the England test cricket team in the 1890s. The church and many of its huddled gravestones were flattened by a landmine on the night of 14 November 1940. My own father witnessed this event and was himself blown unconcious by the blast which killed four young fire-watchers and the assistant curate. The vicar, the Revd John Lister, was seriously injured.

THE CATHEDRAL CHURCH OF ST MICHAEL dates largely from the fourteenth and fifteenth centuries. The original chapel which existed in 1138 probably stood where the south porch is opposite St Mary's Hall. The present building, up until it became a cathedral in 1918, was the largest parish church in England in length and height. After its elevation its spire still remains the third tallest in England measuring some three hundred feet. The tower was built between 1373 and 1394, paid for by benefactors William and Adam Botoner, and the steeple was added some years later by their sisters Mary and Anne.

THE BEAUTIFUL INTERIOR OF ST MICHAEL'S in 1939, a year before it was transformed into a pile of smouldering rubble. It is said that Sir Christopher Wren came here in the 1660s and declared the building an architectural masterpiece. Within these vast arches was contained a treasure house of Coventry's history in stone, wood, alabaster, brass and glass.

THE MAGNIFICENT EAST WINDOW AND CHANCEL of St Michael's before its destruction. Now, despite being but a shell, the tracery has survived and is still recognizable. Below the window of the ruins is now carved the words 'Father Forgive' in front of which stands a simple stone altar made from the rubble on which was erected the famous charred cross made from burnt roof beams.

A REREDOS INSTALLED IN ST MICHAEL'S in 1860. The sections represent the sacrifices of Abel, Noah, Melchisedec, Abraham and the Last Supper. This was just one of many sculptures and monuments from many centuries which were destroyed when the blazing roof of the cathedral collapsed into the main structure.

THE LADY OR DRAPER'S CHAPEL in 1912. The chapel, nicknamed 'the chapel on the Mount', because of its great height above ground level, was actually built upon the charnel-house of the church, where bones and skulls were stored from the overfull churchyard. The chapel was on the left of the east window.

THE WEEKLY BREAD DOLE in St Michael's around 1910. This practice of the weekly distribution of bread lasted for over three hundred years. The bread distributed at this time was paid for by charities founded by James Harwell in 1630, Thomas Jesson in 1636, Simon Norton in 1641 and Humphrey Burton in 1683. By the time this photograph was taken there were few who wished to take advantage of this ancient charity.

THE MORNING OF 15 NOVEMBER 1940. The old cathedral of St Michael's lies in ruins after a night of destruction by the German Luftwaffe who laid the city centre to waste. The Revd Richard Howard, Mr Jack Forbes, Mr W. Eaton and Mr White fought valiantly half the night with what little was at hand, as large numbers of incendiary bombs fell continuously upon the roof. After incendiaries took hold in the eighteen-inch roof space the battle was lost and after saving what they could from the burning interior these brave fire-fighters had to stand back and watch as the great building collapsed among great red flames which licked the sky.

THE TOP OF BAYLEY LANE in the 1860s, showing No. 22, a sixteenth-century cottage, now a solicitors. In the background stands St Mary's Hall, considered to be one of the finest guildhalls in the country.

THIS VIEW UP BAYLEY LANE with St Mary's Hall on the left and St Michael's south porch on the right was taken on a bright morning in June 1933. The scene has changed little, except for the loss of the lamp. Beyond No. 22 the pretty Victorian St Michael's baptist chapel has also gone, gutted by bombs. Later used as a static water-tank, the site is now under renewed construction.

THE COURTYARD OF ST MARY'S HALL from Bayley Lane photographed in the 1890s and unchanged to this day. The guildhall was built in the late fourteenth and early fifteenth centuries as a base for the city's powerful merchant guilds. In the vaulted entrance porch can be seen fine medieval carvings, including a green man with foliage sprouting from his mouth.

THE COURTYARD looking towards the main entrance. The entrance to the main building is on the right under the timbered upper storey which was once used by the drapers guild. The building, apart from being used for civic occasions, was, up until recent years, used as one of the city courts. Those who pass through the entrance today do so voluntarily.

ST MARY'S GREAT HALL in 1898, like the rest of the building unchanged. The hall boasts a medieval decorated truss-roof, full-size portraits of various English monarchs, stained-glass windows, armour and a minstrels' gallery. Along the passageway which leads into this great hall is a huge fifteenth-century tapestry on which can be seen the likeness of Henry VI, a regular visitor to the city. The hall was used as a place of entertainment since its erection. In the eighteenth century it was a regular theatre venue.

THE PRINCE'S CHAMBER, probably used by the trinity guild and later as a second council chamber. The oak panelling and oak Jacobean fire surround were taken from the old Craven Arms in the High Street.

BAYLEY LANE as it turns towards Earl Street in around 1870. On the left is St Michael's and on the right the Drapers Hall. The other buildings are now all gone, bombed and bulldozed away. The building in the centre stood on the site of the new tourist information centre and its medieval cellar has now been opened to the public.

CONTINUING FROM THE LAST PHOTO-GRAPH, this one taken in 1900 shows the end of Bayley Lane. The buildings are now gone and on the left now stands the city record office and museum. Excavations behind the site of these buildings recently revealed medieval workshops and part of the city's defensive and mysterious Red Ditch.

THE GOLDEN CROSS INN, on the corner of Hay and Pepper Lane, photographed around 1930. Tradition says that the inn stands on the site of the old city mint, which for a short period between 1466 and 1470 struck the now rare Coventry groats, nobles and half-nobles bearing the image of King Edward IV. As an inn it dates back to the seventeenth century and was much restored in the mid-nineteenth century, mainly using large oak timbers taken from St Michael's old bell-frame. The buildings behind it in Pepper Lane which included other timbered buildings are now gone.

SECTION SIX

The Great Butcher Row

GREAT BUTCHER ROW looking north in the 1870s.

790 Butcher Row, Coventry.

GREAT BUTCHER ROW, one of Coventry's most well remembered, photographed, drawn and painted streets, which ran along the line of the present Trinity Street down to the steps up to Priory Row. Its lower section, the Bull Ring, continued past this point to New Buildings. The row was once the home of the city's butchers and was known as the Great Butchery. First mentioned in 1309, the row held one of the city's main markets until the 1860s. This lovely street, full of overhanging gables, carved barge boards and corner-posts, oak in abundance and blood-red Elizabethan bricks, would have been one of the city's greatest tourist attractions, had it survived.

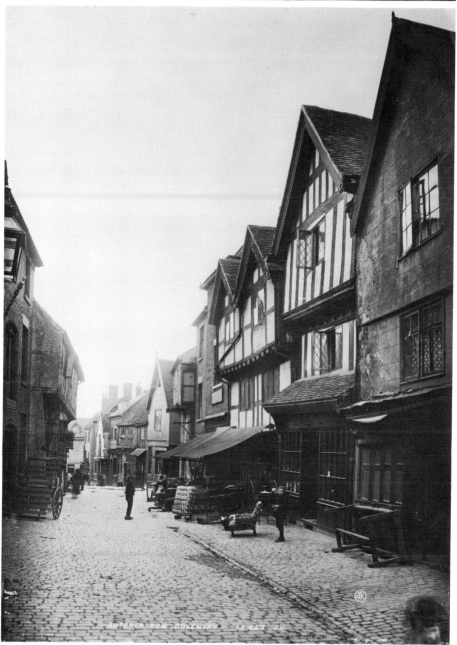

BUTCHER ROW in 1900. The buildings on the right down to the last pointed gable stood where the flower-bed now lies before Holy Trinity church. This amazing view had changed little in nearly four hundred years.

THE CORNER OF BUTCHER ROW AND PRIORY ROW photographed on 24 May 1914. The Elizabethan building on the left was later replaced with a larger mock-Tudor building occupied by Timothy Whites. The site is now occupied by a fast-food restaurant. The three-storeyed timbered building on the right marks the beginning of the present flower-bed.

AROUND THE CORNER INTO PRIORY ROW. This view taken in 1890 is still recognizable to this day, except of course for the disappearance of the far cottage and Butcher Row, seen at the end of the row. The timbered cottage on the right which still thankfully stands was once called Lych Gate House and is thought to have been built by the Revd John Bryan, vicar of Holy Trinity around the year 1648. The cottage was built upon one of the old tower bases of the priory which stood on this site; previously a butcher had kept pigs in the tower base. Bryan had converted the opposing double tower base which still exists behind off New Buildings into two dwellings. Many existing remains of the ancient priory were removed and Bryan had a garden laid out, and later the site gained a bowling green. The lane itself probably led to the Bishops Palace in medieval times and it gained its present straightness when it was relined in 1807. Along the whole length of the lane under ground lies the remains of the old Benedictine Priory.

TRINITY LANE in May 1933. This narrow lane was in fact the back of the houses in Butcher Row. The paved alley follows the line of the present narrow roadway before Holy Trinity Church. At the end of the lane can be seen the cottage in Priory Row.

CITY HISTORIAN J.B. SHELTON studies the remains of the massive priory cathedral church of St Mary's which were discovered during the demolition of an unsafe building on the site late in 1856, shortly after the completion of nearby Blue Coat School. This area was originally the front of the church, likened to Salisbury cathedral, with the far end of the building being next to the new cathedral. The priory, with its huge grounds stretching down to Pool Meadow, was said to have been founded by Lady Godiva and Earl Leofric, both of whom legend says are buried here. The building was dedicated on 4 October 1043 and soon became a rich monastic place of pilgrimage, for here were kept relics such as a bone from St George's arm; a piece of the true cross; the arms of St Augustine, St Jerome and St Justin; a rib of St Lawrence; St Cicely's foot; a piece of the tomb of the Virgin Mary; and a relic of the martyred Thomas of Canterbury. The abbey's history is rich and varied, here murder was done as the abbot and a group of monks were axed to death in the night by a secret assailant. Two English parliaments were held here and kings and queens stayed and worshipped here; Prince Henry, later the famous Henry V, was even arrested here. This great three-spired cathedral church was dismantled by command of King Henry VIII in his second dissolution of the monastaries in 1539. The abbot surrendered the buildings to the king's commissioners and all the brethren left with heads held low.

AN ELIZABETHAN TIMBER BUILDING at the junction of Butcher Row and the Bull Ring photographed around 1900 when serving as a hardware shop. This building stood just below and opposite to the entrance to Priory Row.

THE SPOTTED DOG INN in the Bull Ring at the bottom of Butcher Row, between Priory Row and New Buildings. The Spotted Dog was built in the eighteenth century on the site of the old priory's main entrance. The site is now occupied by H. Samuel. Here in 1424 the council ordered the making of a bull-ring so that the nearby butchers could bait bulls before slaughtering. The Bull Ring suffered the same fate as Butcher Row. Directly above the Atkinson sign is the tower of Holy Trinity church.

LITTLE BUTCHER ROW in 1913. This small street, first mentioned in 1410, ran from Butcher Row to Cross Cheaping along the rear of the present Owen Owen. The unusually tall timbered building sold antiques and curiosities for many years.

BUTCHER ROW in December 1935. A few days after this photograph was taken on New Year's Day 1936, both ends of the row were blocked off and Alderman C. Payne, before a small crowd, officially declared the street closed. The shop with the van and canopies was for many years William Franks, Complete House Furnishers.

THE LOWER WHITE BUILDING on the left was the last on the right in the top photograph. To the far left of this building was the entrance to Broadgate by the Royal Vaults. In the mid-foreground is Trinity Lane and to the right the edge of Trinity church. The cobbled road around Trinity and into Broadgate still exists. This view was taken in December 1935, before the area's demolition.

THE PILGRIM'S REST, standing on the corner of Ironmonger Row and Palmer Lane in the 1860s. This inn, built in 1820, occupied the site of an early monastic guesthouse which was frequented by medieval pilgrims who came to pray to the saintly relics held within the nearby priory. In the nearby River Sherbourne, some of which can still be seen, the pilgrim's signs and badges worn by these followers of God were dredged up many years ago. This building was demolished in 1936 to make way for the construction of Trinity Street. During the demolition part of the rear of the inn was found to belong to the original monastic house.

THE SITE OF THE PRESENT SAINSBURYS and the site of the lower half of Trinity Street after the demolition and clearance of the old properties in 1936. In the background can be seen the old fire station, its left-hand side under construction to match the original Victorian right-hand side.

PRIORY ROW COTTAGE STILL STANDS while all around lies in rubble, cleared for the building of Trinity Street in 1936. This is the same view as seen on p. 82. A mock-Tudor building was attached to the cottage to give it its present look.

THE OPENING OF TRINITY STREET in September 1937. The street, which cost £260,400, was declared open from the Broadgate end (above) by the Lord Mayor, Alderman A.H. Barnacle. The group then walked down the street to the bottom where ex-mayor Alderman V. Wyles, who envisaged the street back in 1910, received the ceremonial scissors and opened the lower section. Before cutting the ribbon the alderman referred to the old Butcher Row as a 'blot on the city', but many did not agree.

SECTION SEVEN

Industry

ONE OF THESE 4 HP DAIMLERS was driven from Land's End to John o'Groats in 1897 by the company's first director, Mr Henry Sturmey. The solid-wheeled vehicle carried a notice upon it which stated that 'the top speed is fourteen miles per hour and the car will not explode'.

THIS PHOTOGRAPH, taken around 1898, shows the birthplace of the British motor car industry. The building, an old cotton mill in Drapers Fields off Sandy Lane, Radford, was converted into a factory to make Daimler, Pennington and Bollee System autocars. The first company to occupy the building was the Great Horseless Carriage Company established in 1896. The company had 200 workers and never produced a car. It was actually set up to establish a franchise while awaiting the repeal of the Red Flag Act which limited the speed of any road-using vehicle. In 1897 it became the Motor Manufacturing Company and the production of Daimler-based cars and motorcycles got under way. In 1905 the Motor Company moved to Parkside, leaving the rapidly growing factory in the hands of the Daimler Motor Company. The original factory stood next to the canal arm and quickly expanded by 1922 to cover all the present area in Sandy Lane now occupied by the East Midlands Electricity Board, industrial units and Kalmar Climax. The main gate was next to the present Kalmar Climax offices in the bend of the road. Built in 1909, these were originally the Daimler offices. Kalmar Climax will shortly be leaving the site.

TO CELEBRATE THE ABOLITION OF THE RED FLAG ACT, which made it illegal to travel over four miles per hour without being preceded by a man carrying a red flag, a car rally was organized. Daimler used this first British car rally from Coventry to Birmingham to promote the brand new Daimler motor car. The rally began in Warwick Road, and in the background can be seen The Quadrant, unchanged to this day. Unconnected with the motor car but still of interest is the fact that No. 1 The Quadrant was, until her death in 1947, the home of Angela Brazil, the world-famous writer of schoolgirl novels.

WORKERS LEAVING the Coventry Daimler works through the Drapers Fields Gate around 1910. There were two other gates into the site from Sandy Lane. These works were not entirely vacated until 1937.

THE DAIMLER ASSEMBLY LINE IN 1947. This photograph was taken at the Radford Plant, at the top of Sandy Lane by Daimler Road. The factory built on Stripes Farm came into use in 1908, quickly becoming the main plant long before the old one down the lane fell into disuse. The plant is now (1991) in its eighty-third year of production and is known locally as the Jag Daimler. The Daimler company is just one of many motor manufacturers which turned Coventry into Car City in the 1960s.

THE JAMES STARLEY MEMORIAL in Queen's Grove, next to the Queens Road Baptist church. James Starley, the son of a Sussex farmer, ran away from home with a wish to improve the world with his inventive genius. His early obsession with an improved rat-trap and self-rocking cradle gave but a small idea of his later inventiveness. He came to Coventry in the summer of 1861. The city's weaving industry had just collapsed and Starley's establishment of the Coventry Sewing Machine Company in King Street helped to drag the city out of its enforced depression. Starley, with his partner William Hillman, would later import the first French velocipedes into the country. Starley turned the boneshaker into the first true cycle, experimenting at his home in Well Street. His improvements included the first complete lightweight metal-framed bike, tightenable cross-spokes and, among fifteen other patents, the differential gear which is found in all vehicles to this day. From these small beginnings Coventry became the largest bicycle producer in the world. Just before his death in the summer of 1881 at the age of fifty-one Starley, by royal command, personally presented Queen Victoria with two of his Salvo Quad cycles. So admired was 'Old Man Starley' for his genius and for the wealth he had brought to ailing Coventry that it was decided a monument should be erected to honour him. This was done after raising £336 by public subscription and the monument was unveiled before a crowd of eight thousand people in Queens Grove. The monument was moved to Warwick Row when the ring-road was constructed in the 1960s.

COVENTRY-MADE 'ORDINARIES' or 'Penny Farthings' in an early photograph. These incredible machines, which had front wheels measuring up to eighty-four inches, could in expert hands reach speeds up to and over twenty miles per hour. James Starley, when he left the Coventry Sewing Machine Company and went into partnership with Hillman, took out his own patent on a penny farthing-type cycle called the Ariel. This bike, produced from 1870, was the world's first all-metal lightweight bicycle. The cycle industry in Coventry grew to include many names such as Rudge, Rudge-Whitworth, Singer, Swift, Rover, Humber, Hillman, Dunlop, BSA and Coventry Eagle, to name but a few. The bicycle is no longer manufactured in the city. The photograph shows, from left to right, Walter Browett, William Thackhall Browett and Alexander Percy Pridmore after their ride from Coventry to Land's End and back on their Coventry Machinist bicycles. The ride, which began on 16 August 1875, was a leisurely one apart from the last day when the three cyclists covered 87 miles.

THE SINGER BICYCLE FACTORY in Canterbury Street in 1896. Established by George Singer in 1874, the company began by producing cycles, then motorcycles, soon following in 1905 with the production of its first motor car. The company ceased motorcycle production after the Second World War and concentrated on producing motor cars, quickly earning itself a reputation in the motoring world. The company was bought by the Rootes Group in 1956.

PROBABLY THE FIRST EVER RACE between a motorbike and a bicycle took place here in the Butts Stadium on 3 August 1897. The motorbike is on the right.

SMITH & SONS, one of many watch-making firms in the city. Watch and clock-making began in the city in the mid-seventeenth century. Coventry's oldest established firm was Rotherhams of Spon Street, founded in 1750 and still in production up until recent years.

PLAYERS WORKSHOP in the Butts specialized in hand-crafted watches. The creation of such crafted watches thrived in the city until the production of cheap machine-made Swiss and American watches ruined the more specialized handmade watch trade. Coventry watches were so finely crafted that it was said they were made to last a hundred years.

THOMAS STEVENS established a silk-weaving business in 1854 just before the industry collapsed. In 1862 he patented an invention which would make his company a success while others failed. His idea was to produce pictorial bookmarks and ribbons. Soon he developed the framed silk picture showing historical scenes, famous individuals etc, which were called Stevengraphs. These became extremely popular and were exhibited throughout the world. They are now considered valuable collectors' items on both sides of the Atlantic. The Stevengraph Factory in Cox Street continued producing Stevengraphs for years after Stevens's death in October 1888.

A STEVENGRAPH called simply 'Coventry'. The Stevengraph factory had literally thousands of these silks stored in its basement after they became less popular. This valuable pile of silk went up in flames during the blitz when the factory was destroyed. Cash's now carry on where Stevens left off.

TWO GENERATIONS WORKING THE LOOMS at Oakey & Cox in Queen Street, photographed in 1948. Although the silk-weaving industry, which was introduced into the city at the beginning of the eighteenth century, finally collapsed in 1860, there were some survivors who employed large numbers of people into the 1950s. Oakey & Cox was under the sole management in 1938 of Mr H. Oakey who supervised the company's production of quality masonic regalia, medal ribbons, hat bands and woven name tags.

SECTION EIGHT

The City at War

MEMBERS OF THE WARWICKSHIRE RIFLE VOLUNTEERS (Coventry Division) at Stoneleigh Deer Park Camp in 1883. The rifle volunteers were the territorials of their day.

A VERY RARE PHOTOGRAPH taken around 1875 showing men of the Royal Field Artillery stationed at the old Coventry barracks. The barracks, which was built on land belonging to the historic Bull's Head in Smithford Street, came into use in 1793. Coventry had been a military city for some time, with men being billeted around the many city inns. The first occupants of the newly-built barracks were the newly-formed Coventry Volunteers, part of a large volunteer movement set up to repulse a threatened invasion from France. Before 1800 and up to the 1860s regiments of Cavalry, Dragoons, Hussars and Lancers were stationed here. Next came regiments of the Royal Artillery, followed by the Seventh Battalion of the Royal Warwickshire Regiment who were stationed here before leaving for France in the First World War. Men who paraded daily on this parade ground fought battles throughout the world for 120 years. Coventry Corporation bought the barracks in 1920 and a market was opened on the parade ground in June 1922. It soon became known as the Barracks Market and remained in use until shortly after the Second World War. The site is now mainly occupied by the Barracks car park. The two buildings on the right were part of a row which formed either side of the entrance from Smithford Street, they were later demolished and replaced by the well-remembered City Arcade. The rear entrance to the barracks was from the bottom of Hertford Street, by what we now call the Bull Yard. The long building is one of the stable-blocks later demolished to make way for British Home Stores.

REVIEWING THE COVENTRY DIVISION of the Warwickshire Rifle Volunteers in 1880. Scenes such as this were common in the city for over two hundred years.

A MILITARY FUNERAL passing through Broadgate before the First World War. The soldiers belong to the Seventh Battalion of the Royal Warwickshire Regiment. Soon would come the Great War and death would reign over Europe.

PART OF THE MASSIVE RED LANE ORDNANCE FACTORY just before the outbreak of the First World War. The men are fulfilling a naval contract to supply fifteen-inch guns for naval destroyers. The works at this period employed three thousand men. After the outbreak of war the factory was greatly enlarged and the workforce grew with it. So large in fact was the workforce that more homes were needed. This need was fulfilled by the building of a huge housing estate at Stoke Heath. This factory employed both men and women producing armaments including guns, shells, bullets and aeroplanes. It is believed that the first ever tank was produced in this factory. The army, however, could not at the time be convinced that the vehicle would be of any use on the battlefield, but their opinion would soon change. To protect these huge works from possible air attack from German zeppelins, fourteen soldiers were posted here armed with a tiny wheeled cannon which was constantly kept pointing at the sky. There was in fact little to worry about as the first zeppelin raid on the Midlands was not very impressive; its casualties were a cow, a sheep and a medium-sized tree.

THE ROYAL WARWICKSHIRE REGIMENT was formed by order of William III in 1688. Since then the regiment has fought in all major campaigns with honour. As Coventry has always been in Warwickshire (despite electoral boundaries), the men of the city generally joined the county regiment. The photograph shows my own grandfather, Walter McGrory (left), and a comrade in arms, just two of the twenty-five thousand Coventry men who fought in the First World War. Walter enlisted under-age in the Second Regiment of the Royal Warwicks and fought with the regiment at Gallipoli, Cape Helles, Sulva Bay, Gallipoli again, Ginchy, Arras and Cambrai. During these campaigns he received fifteen wounds and was gassed twice. In May 1918, after receiving a gold and silver cigarette case from his captain for helping to hold off a German force while outnumbered for five days, Walter was sent back to the front. Luckily he survived the horrors of the trenches and returned to his home in Court Three, Hill Street, opposite Bablake.

THE IRISH MUNSTER FUSILIERS arrived in the city on 11 January 1915 straight from India. The photograph shows them on Pool Meadow waiting to be billeted around the city. The Irishmen's humour and geniality warmed the hearts of Coventrians who presented the regiment with a scroll of thanks for their friendship.

THE MUNSTERS marching down Hertford Street, now wearing normal uniforms, their destination Gallipoli. This was a one-way trip for some of Coventry's favourite Irishmen. The *Coventry Graphic* regularly reported on the fate of the men of this regiment, some of whom returned to marry Coventry girls. The tallest building in the background is the post office, now minus its top floor. The building on the left is Johnson & Mason's Wine and Spirit Merchants. To the right of the post office is the Coventry Savings Bank and the Queen's Head Hotel, both of which were destroyed in the Second World War.

THE TANK BANK WEEK PARADE passing from Cross Cheaping into Broadgate in 1918. The tank was brought to the city to spearhead a national campaign to raise money for the war effort. This was the first tank ever seen in the streets of Coventry and it made quite an impact. To commemorate the event Goss China produced small china copies of the tank bearing the city arms. These were sold locally in shops such as David Burdett's in Cross Cheaping. The tank ended its money-raising tour of the city on Greyfriars Green where it was used as a platform for fund-raising speakers.

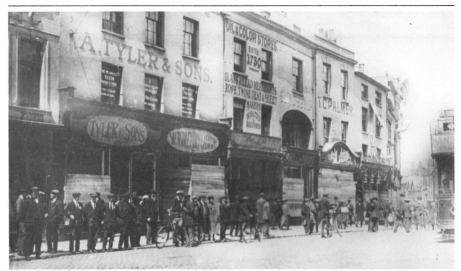

AFTER THE GODIVA PEACE PROCESSION of 1919. This view was taken after three nights of rioting in the city centre, which began on the night of the Godiva procession on Saturday 18 June. Continuous police baton charges finally put an end to the riots which it was said were started by rumours that certain shops in Broadgate were German-held. Others suggested that they were due to the fact that Godiva had ridden through the streets fully clothed. See also p. 59.

THE WAR MEMORIAL being unveiled in the newly-opened War Memorial Park by Field Marshal Earl Haig before fifty thousand people on 8 October 1927. In a hushed silence he placed a roll of honour containing the names of 2,587 Coventry men who fell in the Great War in the monument's inner chamber of silence. On the left stands Dr Lisle Carr, bishop of Coventry, and Frederick Smith, town clerk and city historian.

AFTER A SHORT PEACE the world was once again at war. The young men of Coventry left their native city to fight on foreign shores, leaving the city's war production in the capable hands of their fathers, mothers, wives, daughters and girlfriends. This war, however, would be different to the last for, on the night of 14 November 1940, a clear hunters' moon in the sky, a deep drone was heard. It was seven o'clock in the evening and soon fires began to rage amid great explosions in the city's heart. This was a new kind of warfare; the mass bombing of civilian targets. By 6.16 the next morning Coventry lay in ruins. Amid these ruins 554 people lay dead and 865 injured. The German Luftwaffe had indiscriminately rained down a massive 500 tons of high explosives and 30,000 incendiary bombs upon the city's heart, destroying and damaging 46,000 homes and 75 per cent of the city's industry. The world had never before witnessed such massive overnight devastation and the Germans coined a new word for this destruction, 'Coventrated'. This shows Broadgate with Cross Cheaping on the left and Trinity Street on the right on the morning of 15 November. The building in the centre was the fairly new Owen Owen store, now completely gutted.

THE RIGHT-HAND SIDE OF BROADGATE, looking down past Trinity church into Trinity Street. After the night of destruction shocked Coventrians wandered around the city viewing the devastation with disbelief. Many who had spent the night on the outskirts of the city heard the great rumbling throughout the night and watched the sky glowing above the city. Despite this, many headed for their jobs in the morning, only to find their place of work had ceased to exist.

TWO PHOTOGRAPHS SHOWING CROSS CHEAPING the morning after the 'Big Raid'. The burnt-out wreckage of three-quarters of the city's bus fleet lay scattered around the city. On the left of the bus wreckage is the shell of the old Owen Owen store. The present store now stands here. Armed soldiers began to appear as six hundred were drafted into the city to keep order and help with the continuing search for bodies among the ruins.

THIS PHOTOGRAPH SHOWS HERTFORD STREET still ablaze on the morning of 15 November 1940. The view, looking towards Broadgate, shows firemen tackling a blaze which is engulfing the Queen's Head, the National Savings Bank and the main post office. During the previous night twenty-six firemen had been killed and two hundred injured amid the blazing city. The night had been one of great heroism, not only among the services, but also among the people of Coventry. The firemen are standing practically in front of the post office which survived the war.

FIRE SERVICE AND AUXILIARY MEN have a well-earned cup of tea at a mobile canteen, one of many set up around the city the morning after the 'Big Raid'. After a night of horror smiles could still be found among the city's resilient inhabitants.

A RESCUE PARTY pose amid the rubble-strewn corner of Sandy Lane and Daimler Road, Radford. On the left of this photograph taken on 15 November lies the Daimler factory, a Luftwaffe target of the previous night. The factory had taken a number of direct hits from high explosives which did serious damage but did not stop the factory assembling aero engines. Many bombs overshot and landed on the common and odd houses. The building in the background (left) is now, and has been for many years, a corner shop.

THE MOST POWERFUL SYMBOL of the city's destruction was the old cathedral church of St Michael. This evocative photograph, which shows the hinges of the great west door standing out against the skyline, was taken in the afternoon of 15 November. The many people who came to the ruins stood stunned among the rubble. On the following day the King himself (George VI) walked around the ruins, then made a tour of the city to boost Coventrians' morale.

CHRISTCHURCH, BY GREYFRIARS GREEN, was hit during the 8 April raid in 1941 which many say was more concentrated than that of 14 November. The main body of the church was gutted, leaving only the tower and spire standing, alone for the second time in the history of the church. The remains of the body of the church were pulled down in 1950. During the night bombs also hit St Mary's Hall, St John's and St Mark's. Factories were hit and the Coventry and Warwickshire hospital was rendered virtually unusable. This and other raids in April brought the city's death toll to 1,200, with 1,746 injured.

WAR HERO VISCOUNT MONTGOMERY OF ALAMEIN reviews members of the Royal Warwickshire Regiment in the War Memorial Park shortly after receiving the freedom of the city on behalf of the regiment. On the left of Monty in this photograph taken on 31 May 1947 is the mayor, Alderman G. Briggs. Later in the afternoon the Royal Warwicks paraded through the city centre and Monty took the salute at the main door of the Council House. Monty's staff car was built in Coventry at Humber-Hillman.

The Phoenix Rises

NEW UNION STREET under construction around 1957. In the background can be seen the Cheylesmore labour exchange.

BROADGATE in 1941. The rubble has been cleared away leaving large open areas in the city centre. On the far left can be seen the columns of the present-day National Westminster bank, the only building remaining from pre-war Broadgate. Right of the bank is the old Martin's Bank, more recently a branch of the Coventry Economic Building Society. This building, which survived the wrath of the Luftwaffe, fell to the developers in 1990. The white building on the corner of Broadgate and Smithford Street was the Burtons building, behind which the present Broadgate House stands. On the right stands the old market clock tower, now the site of the Hotel Leofric. Most of Broadgate in front of the Burtons building is now covered by Cathedral Lanes. Compare this view with that at the top of p. 19 which shows the Burtons building on the left.

THE NATIONAL PROVINCIAL BANK on the corner of the High Street and Hertford Street overlooking Broadgate. This view, taken in the late 1940s, shows what was to become James Walker's shop set into the bottom right of the building. Walker's are still here in an extension to the building. Other shops are set within the side of the bank, now the National Westminster. A sweet shop which began operating when the bank first opened is still trading, a reminder of old Hertford Street.

TEMPORARY SHOPS on the east side of Broadgate, taken in 1949. This point, at which many disembarked from the city's buses, remained the same until the 1960s. The whole of this site, including Broadgate in front, now lies under Cathedral Lanes.

THE FIRST STAGE OF BROADGATE'S REDEVELOPMENT gets under way with the opening of the new enlarged island Broadgate. The opening ceremony in May 1948 was performed by the future Queen, Princess Elizabeth.

BROADGATE in October 1949, showing the newly unveiled Lady Godiva statue sculpted in bronze by Sir William Reid Dick and paid for by Mr Bassett Green. The unveiling ceremony was performed by Mrs Lewis Douglas, wife of the American Ambassador to the Court of Saint James, a few days earlier on 22 October. Note in the background the site of the present Owen Owen store with Trinity Street on the right.

THE QUEEN MOTHER (then the Queen) on a visit to Coventry with King George VI on 5 April 1951. Left to right: John Howat (mayor), Harry Weston (deputy mayor), Queen Elizabeth and, behind them, Lord and Lady Willoughby de Broke.

LOOKING FROM HOLY TRINITY towards the west side of Broadgate in 1962. Hertford Street had not yet been pedestrianized and visitors to the Bridge Restaurant could watch buses driving beneath them. This scene remained basically unchanged until the redevelopment in 1990.

J.B. SHELTON MBE (1875–1958) excavating in Broadgate. 'JB', the father of Coventry's archaeological history, was the son of a farm labourer who came to Coventry from Nottingham and worked as a drayman. Later he set himself up successfully in business in Little Park Street. Once his business flourished 'JB' began to indulge his fascination for history. Every hole in the ground made by bombs or bulldozers was explored by 'JB' in his never-ending search for the city's past. He was made City Chamberlain in 1945 and the huge collection of objects he had rescued and documented were put on display in his own Benedictine Museum. These objects, which now form the main basis of the city's collection of ancient objects, were presented to the city by 'JB' in November 1958. The following day he was killed, struck down by a motorbike. His legacy is in the Herbert Art Gallery and Museum for all to see.

THE RUINS OF ST MICHAEL'S and Bayley Lane are practically unchanged since this photograph was taken in the 1940s. The view was taken from the corner, at the junction with Priory Street. Next to the cars can be seen a collapsed brick-lined cellar. Next to this cellar is a fourteenth-century stone vaulted cellar, one of many in the city but the only one to which the public has access, via the new tourist information centre built on this corner site.

KING GEORGE VI AND THE QUEEN leave the now-cleared ruins of the old cathedral church of St Michael during their visit to the city on 5 April 1951. The King is accompanied by John Howat, mayor, and the lady mayoress. During his visit the King had been brought up to date with redevelopment of the city centre and the plans for building a new cathedral, which were of great personal interest to his majesty who had visited the old cathedral two days after its destruction.

LESS THAN TWO YEARS AFTER THE DESTRUCTION OF ST MICHAEL'S it was publicly announced that a new cathedral would be built. The first design intended to be used was by Sir Gilbert Scott. His designs, however, were dropped and an open competition was held. The winner, announced in August 1951, was Basil Spence. It was Spence's idea to build a grand new cathedral attached to the old one upon the former burial ground. The Queen laid the foundation stone of the building on 22 March 1956 and over the following years the great structure grew and grew, a mass of modern art encapsulated in one great monument to God. One of the final acts of the building's completion was the placing of a ninety-foot bronze lattice-work fleche on the roof of the imposing pink Hollington stone nave. This photograph, taken on 26 April 1962 after eight years' construction, shows that final act in progress.

ST MICHAEL'S NEW CATHEDRAL from the south-east, taken in 1965. At the top of the wide stairway can be seen the massive and impressive statue of St Michael defeating the devil. This was the last major work of Sir Jacob Epstein before his death in 1959.

A PHOTOGRAPH TAKEN FROM THE PORCH looking through John Hutton's ethereal glass screen covered with stylized angels. In the background, covering the whole of the north wall, can be seen the largest tapestry in the world entitled *Christ in Glory*. It was the creation of Graham Sutherland and was made in France. The photograph, taken in 1965, shows an orchestral concert in progress.

THE DEVELOPMENT OF THE PRECINCT gets under way. In the background can be seen the rear of the Hotel Leofric built on the market site. This view was taken from Smithford Street and marks the point where the street crosses the precinct, only to disappear under the buildings in the Lower Precinct. The timbered building is the White Lion Inn, the scene of the bloody murder of the inn's landlady and serving-maid in the middle of the eighteenth century. On the left of the inn can be seen the corner of the present Marks & Spencer store.

THE UPPER PRECINCT COMPLETED in what came to be known as 'Festival of Britain' style. The Marks & Spencer store was opened on 2 April 1954.

A VIEW OF THE UPPER PRECINCT, the world's first pedestrian shopping centre. This photograph, taken in 1961, shows the precinct as it was originally envisaged by city architect Donald Gibson, with the spire of St Michael's as the focal point. The first completed building was Broadgate House, opened in May 1953. This was followed three months later by Woolworth, then Marks & Spencer and British Home Stores. Gradually the gaps were filled in to give the above view. Just before the bridge, which now incorporates Zales, is the levelling stone carved with a phoenix rising from the ashes, a symbol of Coventry's rebirth. A few short yards from the left of this stone was Market Street and the birthplace of the great Victorian English actress, Dame Ellen Terry. Much of this thoughtfully conceived view has now been obstructed by a large unattractive escalator constructed to take shoppers into the newly opened (April 1991) West Orchards (there was no 's' in the original spelling) Shopping Centre. The new Cathedral Lanes Shopping Centre also blocks off much of the church tower.

THE CITY 'DRINKWATER' ARCADE in Smithford Street. This arcade with its twenty-four shops formed the entrance to the Barracks Market. It was built on the site of the original entrance to the eighteenth-century army barracks. The arcade suffered minor bomb damage in the war and was demolished during the building of the upper precinct; however, the market to which it led survived.

THE BARRACKS MARKET in June 1948. In the background can be seen the Empire Cinema in Hertford Street. The building, up until recently the ABC Cinema, now lies empty. Further to the left is the spire of Holy Trinity and Smithford Street.

A BUSY DAY inside the covered part of the Barracks Market in the 1950s. The market occupied the old Barracks Square from 1922. Firstly the central area of stalls was uncovered and, although many of the original army buildings were demolished, some were kept and used by the traders. The market entrances via the City Arcade and the Bull Yard at the bottom of Hertford Street were not only part of the original barracks but also of the ancient Bull Inn which stood on the site. The market and its surrounding buildings were finally closed and demolished in November 1958 and the area was turned into the Barracks multi-storey car park.

SECTION TEN

Around the City

THIS POSTCARD from the early 1920s shows the three spires and four views taken around Styvechale.

THIS AMAZING VIEW of St Michael's and Holy Trinity was taken from around Lower Ford Street in 1860. The road in the foreground is Cox Street, and in the background can be seen the newly-constructed Priory Street. Next to the bridge on Priory Street can be seen Reed and Co., harness, reed and slaymakers (with the chimney). The ground on the right is Pool Meadow; behind the photographer lie open fields.

DESPITE THE BLITZ AND EARLIER DEVELOPMENT hundreds of old buildings still existed in post-war Coventry. This photograph taken in Spon Street around 1957 shows the Coventry Movement Company, a small engineering firm established in 1889 as a manufacturer of watch movements. Sadly, the rest of the city's old buildings did not fare as well in the developers' hands as Spon Street did.

ONE OF THE MANY COURTS which could be found throughout the city. This photograph, taken in 1957, shows Court Thirty-eight in Spon Street, one of hundreds of such courts built between the early eighteenth and early nineteenth centuries. My own grandfather and father were born in an older, larger court opposite Bablake School in Hill Street.

HAMMERTON'S IN MUCH PARK STREET around 1957. Hammerton's was established in the 1830s as dyers of ribbons and trimmings. This handsome Elizabethan building with carved barge-boards was previously the home of the Midland Brewery. Neither has survived.

NOS 20 AND 21 JORDAN WELL STREET in 1941. These buildings, which stood below the Herbert Art Gallery and Museum, were torn down like countless other Elizabethan buildings in the city in the 1950s and 1960s. The phoenix had risen, but at a cost.

A RARE EARLY PHOTOGRAPH of Cook Street Gate from the city side. This view of the gate had changed little in over three hundred years since the houses on the left of the gate were incorporated into the remaining wall. The Elizabethan building through the archway was the Old Tower Inn which was presented to the city by the brewery as a building of historic interest. Despite this it was demolished in July 1963. Cook Street Gate itself thankfully still remains, one of only two remaining city gates left from the original twelve main and minor gates which were dotted around the nearly two-and-a-half-mile long city wall, making a massive fortification which, in its time, was considered second only to London. The wall, which took forty years to complete, was begun in 1355. With its defensive ditches it turned Coventry into an impressive stronghold. Mother Shipton the prophetess predicted that a pigeon would cause the great wall to fall. This may sound ridiculous, but in 1662 Charles II ordered that the wall be pulled down for it held his father's army at bay during the Civil War. The breaching and destruction of the wall in 1662 was carried out by the mayor of Coventry, whose name was Pidgeon.

THE OPPOSITE SIDE OF COOK STREET GATE, showing the Old Tower Inn around 1910. The destruction of the surrounding buildings in the early 1960s has left the gate standing alone.

THE CITY WALL running from Cook Street Gate down to Priory or Swanswell Gate. This stretch of the city wall was purchased by Sir Alfred Herbert, engineering giant and city benefactor. It was the intention of Sir Alfred and his wife, Florence, to turn the area into a garden walk for the city, taking in this, the longest section of the city wall. After Lady Herbert's unexpected death in May 1930 Sir Alfred went ahead with the planned garden as a lasting memorial to his late wife. Thus the old Rope Walk, where John Astley established his rope manufacturing yard in 1730, became Lady Herbert's Garden. The buildings in the background, which included Chauntry Place, were demolished in 1934 when the garden was extended.

SWANSWELL OR PRIORY GATE in Hales Street around 1910. Swanswell Gate was built in 1461 to replace another gate which stood at the south end of the old fire station. The gate was built and the course of the city wall altered to take in Swanswell Pool (then a much larger pool known as Swineswell) at the personal request of the Prior of Coventry. In the nineteenth century the gateway was roofed and converted into a cottage, and it was soon converted into a shop, which it remained until around 1930. The gate was presented to the city by Sir Alfred Herbert and restored in 1931/2. At the present moment it serves as an artist's studio and craft shop.

FORD'S HOSPITAL in Greyfriars Lane as it was in 1890. This almshouse was founded by William Ford in 1509 to provide shelter for five aged men and one aged woman. In 1517 William Pisford left money so that more inmates could be taken within the safe haven of the hospital. By the eighteenth century the inmates were exclusively female. As a piece of architecture Ford's Hospital has always been considered one of the finest buildings of its type in the country.

THE COURTYARD OF FORD'S HOSPITAL in 1898. This tranquil geranium-strewn yard looks exactly the same today as it did some four hundred years ago.

FORD'S HOSPITAL took a direct hit from a single bomb just after midnight on 14 October 1940. A warning of what was to come, the bomb smashed through the roof of the warden's room, killing her, a nurse and six of the building's elderly inmates. The building stood damaged for some time before a proper restoration programme could be got under way.

SIR ALFRED HERBERT reopening Ford's Hospital on 18 June 1953. This superb building was restored using tiles and wood from a rear section of the building which was totally destroyed. During the skilled restoration it was discovered that the building was made not only of oak but that a large proportion was teak, a wood of great rarity when used inland, it being more common in coastal districts.

SWANSWELL POOL in 1898. Known by this name since at least 1610, the pool was once much larger but has been reduced in size twice. Legend states that it was formed by the rutting of a giant wild boar which terrorized the area until it was despatched by Sir Guy of Warwick. The pool powered two water mills from medieval times until the nineteenth century, when the southern side was filled in for the building of White Street. In the background can be seen the old Coventry and Warwickshire hospital built in 1864/5 (right) and Victorian St Mark's (left).

FISHING THE SWANSWELL in 1910. In the background stands the city flour mill which ground flour from 1868 to the 1960s.

CHILDREN FISHING THE SWANSWELL through the White Street railings in 1910. Here warm water flowed into the pool from the city flour mill opposite. These children, like those of generations before and after them tried, to catch the large carp which swam around this particularly food-rich area.

THE ORIGINAL SWANSWELL TAVERN, on the corner of Swanswell Street and Primrose Hill, in 1910.

THE COVENTRY CEMETERY on the London Road was designed by Joseph Paxton (later Sir Joseph Paxton) who, at the time, was superintendent of the Duke of Devonshire's gardens at Chatsworth House and the famed designer of the great Crystal Palace, erected in Hyde Park for the Great Exhibition in 1851. Paxton, an MP for Coventry from 1854 to 1865, was also at one time the city's mayor. He personally supervised the laying out of the London Road Cemetery in 1846/7 and erected two chapels among its beautiful landscaped grounds, one Church of England and one Nonconformist. After Sir Joseph's death in 1865 a Gothic monument was erected near the cemetery entrance to commemorate this notable gardener-architect. The landscape grounds soon became a fashionable venue for a Sunday afternoon stroll.

THE HOUSE AND GARDENS of Barr's Hill School, Radford, taken around 1915. Legend states that a Roman general dug fortifications on this raised hill, but the facts are that during the Civil War the city's garrison created an outer 'Barr' here, ditched and defended to keep the Royalist army at bay. In more recent times a house was built here, which became the home of J.K. Starley, cycle manufacturer, owner of the Rover Car Company and nephew of James Starley of Coventry cycle fame (see p. 93). In 1908 the house became the Barr's Hill Girls' School, the first fee-paying secondary school in the city. It remained a single sex school into the early 1970s when it became a comprehensive school. Despite opposition and promises to the contrary, Barr's Hill House was demolished and turned into a car park. Below is the Clock Room.

BLUE COAT SCHOOL, Priory Row, in 1898. The school was founded on this site in 1714, its purpose being to educate girls in the 'important' things in life, namely 'reading, riting, rithmatic' and domestic duties. The fine building in the photograph was the second on the site, built in 1856. After its completion the adjoining building was found to be unsafe and was demolished. During the work pillar bases from the old priory were uncovered and can still be seen. The school was closed in 1940 and reopened as a comprehensive school in Terry Road in 1964. The original school has been used by Coventry City Transport, the Samaritans and Alcoholics Anonymous. The girls' blue uniforms in the photograph below, taken around 1890, are unchanged since the school's foundation 176 years earlier.

BABLAKE SCHOOL DRUM AND FIFE BAND in 1868. These extraordinary school uniforms were based on the original sixteenth-century design. The long tunics were 'Coventry blue' (a dark blue created from sloe berries) with brass buttons, and this style was worn from 1837 to 1889. Bablake still had a band twenty years after this photograph was taken and were in direct competition with Katherine Bayley's Blue Gift School as to which band was musically the best.

INMATES OF FORD'S HOSPITAL in winter dress.

THE BLUE GIFT SCHOOL drum and fife band photographed in their schoolyard in Little Park Street in 1880. This charity school was founded in 1735 by Mrs Katherine Bayley (sometimes Bailey). The school was originally founded for eight boys and eight girls, but it soon became an exclusively boys' school, where the boys were prepared for 'useful occupations'. The gentleman on the left is Mr William George Fretton (1829–1900), who succeeded his father as headmaster of the school from 1856 to 1888, when the school was amalgamated with Bablake School. During his lifetime William Fretton wrote large amounts of material on local history for the *Coventry Herald*, which was later put into book form. One of his first tasks on becoming headmaster of the school was to form his own drum and fife band. The band earned an excellent reputation and they were often called upon to play at public functions. The rivalry between Blue Coat and Bablake was intense until the schools' amalgamation.

MARY ANN EVANS (1819–86), alias novelist George Eliot. Mary Ann may have been born near Nuneaton, but George Eliot the writer was literally born in Coventry. Partly educated here, and a resident for a number of years, Mary Ann was changed from a religious zealot with little interest in writing to a woman of greater depth and understanding of the world around her. It was here that Charles Bray saw her potential and encouraged her to write. This portrait of Mary Ann was painted in Geneva in 1849 after a trip to the continent with the Brays.

CHARLES BRAY in later years. On a winter's morning in November 1841 Mary Ann was introduced to Charles Bray at his home, Rosehill, in Radford (on the site of the Coachmakers Club). Bray, a ribbon weaver, owner of the *Coventry Herald* and self-proclaimed 'free-thinker' had turned Rosehill into an arcadia for other free-thinkers. Mary Ann was infatuated and greatly influenced by Bray, who counted among his friends and visitors to his home many of the period's major writers, philosophers and politicians. Within a month of becoming a regular at Rosehill, Mary Ann disregarded her Christian beliefs and opened her mind to the world. Soon she was writing regular features in Bray's *Coventry Herald*.

NANTGLYN AT THE END OF WARWICK ROW, around 1918. Now George Loveitt's and the Bhooj-Bhaban Restaurant, this building was, in the middle of the nineteenth century, a private school run by Mary and Rebecca Franklin, daughters of the Revd Francis Franklin of the Cow Lane Baptist chapel. It was here, from the age of thirteen to sixteen, that Mary Ann Evans was educated, and modelled herself upon 'Miss Rebecca' who had acquired 'Parisian' manners while staying in France. Here, also, her religious zeal was fed.

BIRD GROVE at the bottom of the present George Eliot Road, Foleshill. Much changed now, this photograph shows how it looked in the nineteenth century when purchased by Robert Evans, Mary Ann's father. Here Mary Ann kept house for her father from 1841 until his unexpected death in 1849, when she was thirty. After his death Mary Ann left the house and stayed with the Brays before moving to London to expand her growing literary career. In 1958 the building was converted into a Mormon chapel, then later a temple for the local Asian community.

COVENTRY FAIR on Pool Meadow in the 1920s. Pool Meadow was once a very large mill pool known as St Osburg's Pool and later as the Mill Dam. The mill which this large sheet of water served was known as the Priory Mill, and its wheel turned from early medieval times to the late 1840s, when it was demolished, its dam removed and the water culverted. This resulted in the pool turning into something resembling a swamp. When the city council was seeking an alternative permanent site for the Coventry Fair, which had previously been held on Greyfriars Green, they decided that the old pool site, properly drained, would be ideal. The drainage was carried out and the Great Fair was thereafter held annually on Pool Meadow from 1859 to 1930, when it was moved to Barras Heath, then Hearsall Common. The large Victorian building in the background was the Priory Street Baths, and further to the right the old slay mill can be seen, its chimney lying next to the River Sherbourne. Behind it is the old Triumph factory.

THE MARTYRS' MEMORIAL in 1929, seen next to the junction of Mile Lane and Quinton Road. The memorial, erected in 1910, was moved from this spot during the construction of the ring-road. The memorial commemorates the burning at the stake of eleven religious martyrs in the sixteenth century. The site of the execution was over two hundred yards away from the present memorial site in the Park Hollows, an old shallow quarry which formed a natural amphitheatre.

THE CORNER OF COW LANE AND CHEYLESMORE (behind the present Hare and Squirrel) in 1929. The house on the corner was called Park James Cottage. Park James was keeper of Park Gardens and Cheylesmore Estate. The timbered building above it is the Hare and Squirrel, run by Arthur Petty. Cow Lane was widened in 1927 and demolished in phases in 1937 to 1948 and the 1950s. Many of the buildings dated from the fifteenth and sixteenth centuries.

A RECOGNIZABLE VIEW OF HALES STREET around 1905. On the end of the street with the chimney can be seen the Grammar School, a large part of which was demolished during the construction of this street in 1848. Along from the Grammar School (right, next to the tram) can be seen the Opera House which was built in 1889. In this 2,000-seater building the people of Coventry were entertained with films and live shows, such as plays, musicals and dramas. The exterior was revamped in 1935 and a false frontage added. The old Opera House was demolished in 1961. The building nearest on the right still stands although the lower section has been refronted. The buildings on the opposite side of the road from the Opera House are still standing today as the shops of small traders.

A SCENE OF DEVASTATION; not after the blitz this time, but before. This is the result of clearance work in 1929 for the construction of Corporation Street (opened 1931). Many courts, shops, workshops and factories once occupied this area between Well Street and West Orchard. This view, from the bottom of Chapel Street (itself demolished), shows the tower of St John's and the area demolished, which was much larger than that needed for Corporation Street.

THE REX CINEMA in Corporation Street. (On the opposite corner now stands the *Coventry Evening Telegraph* offices.) This impressive white-fronted cinema was opened by Mayor Barnacle on Monday 8 February 1937. Less than four years later, on 14 November 1940, it was completely gutted by bombs. The next film scheduled to be shown was, appropriately, *Gone with the Wind*. The site later became the Rex Market, then Boots and adjoining shops.

TRAM CONDUCTORS IN BROADGATE in 1915. Women were desperately needed to fill the jobs of men who had gone to war. The lady third from left was the city's first lady conductress. It is interesting to note that only one man in the background is in forces uniform. Within two years practically every man in the street would be in uniform. The road in the background is Market Place.

TRAM NO. 55 in Broadgate in 1932. In the background is the familiar National Provincial (now Westminster) Bank.

THE FREE LIBRARY in 1898, renamed the Gulson Library in 1917 after city mayor John Gulson who presented the site to the city and paid for much of the building. The part in the photograph, with its Cuckoo Lane entrance, was the reference section, containing twenty thousand books. This was completely destroyed in the blitz, leaving the remaining section to serve as the city's central library until it was demolished to make way for the present Cathedral Lanes shopping centre.

NAULS MILL PARK, Radford around 1910. The pool began life as a mill pond serving a water mill which stood here until its demolition in 1889. The area was later laid out as a park and became extremely popular with Coventrians. From the beginning of the twentieth century, up until 1953, military bands played here regularly on evenings and weekends. The bandstand in the background was dismantled in 1963.

A PEELER IN THE DOORWAY of the old Watch House, photographed in the 1850s. The Watch House (a police box with cells) stood next to the Women's Market House on the site of the present Hotel Leofric. This eighteenth-century three-storied building served as a temporary lock-up and resting place for the city constables (watchmen). The plumbing in this building left a lot to be desired and earnt it the nickname of the Bog House Prison. The stocks, which were normally occupied by drunks, were moved from next to the Market Hall to the nearby Watch House in 1840. Here they stood until the Watch House fell from use in 1865 when a new police station was opened in St Mary's Lane. The stocks were later re-erected in 1900 as a purely decorative feature in the alleyway next to St Mary's Hall. In 1929 they were removed and stored in the hall's vaults.

THE KNAVE'S POST stood in a wall niche in Much Park Street for over two hundred years. It began life as a whipping post to which criminals would be tied and flogged. From the eighteenth century it was placed in a high niche. The second niche it occupied (see photograph) was found to be too shallow and the oak figure had to be reduced in thickness to fit. Petty criminals, including women and children, were punished by being tied to the tail of a cart and whipped from the Mayor's Parlour in Cross Cheaping to the Knave's Post and back.

A RARE VIEW OF COVENTRY GAOL in Cuckoo Lane, photographed in the late 1860s. The gaol next to Trinity church had stood here since the seventeenth century and was rebuilt on a number of occasions. This was the home of murderers and pickpockets until the last prisoner left on 20 July 1860. It was against this wall that Mary Ball was hanged amid a sea of people for poisoning her husband in 1849. The gaol was demolished in around 1871 to make way for the building of the Free Library.

THE ANNUAL POLICE INSPECTION at the Coventry Barracks on Monday 21 June 1915. More than two hundred and fifty police officers and special constables are being inspected down to their whistles and notebooks by the chief inspector of the constabulary, Mr Leonard Dunning. The special constables in the background dressed in civilian clothes were to replace a large number of police officers who had been released for army service. These police officers were stationed at the police station on the corner of St Mary's Lane and Bayley Lane. The present headquarters in Little Park Street was officially opened in 1957.

ON THE MORNING OF 31 DECEMBER 1900 some Coventrians woke up to scenes like this. The River Sherbourne burst its banks and those living in low-lying parts of the city found themselves under water. The areas in these photographs, Spon Street (above) and Fleet Street, and the bottom of Smithford Street (below) were, in the distant past, part of a great shallow lake and flood plain. St John's church, seen on the left of the horse-cart in the top photograph, actually recorded a depth of five-and-a-half feet within the church itself.

COVENTRY STATION in 1874. The stationary train is a LNWR 'Bloomer' class engine called *Apollo*. The station, which lies on the Birmingham to London line, was opened in 1838 and was laid out by George Stephenson, who personally walked the proposed route of the railway three times. When the line first opened, the fare to London, a six-hour journey was £1 7s. 6d. By 1910 the journey had been cut to two hours. In the background can be seen the Railway Inn, now The Rocket.

THE EATON ROAD ENTRANCE to Coventry Station around 1905. In 1871 H.W. Eaton (who became Lord of the Manor of Cheylesmore in 1887) purchased the old Coventry Park Estate, which stretched from Greyfriars Green to Quinton Pool, from the Marquis of Hertford. He gave land to build a new access road to the station. This road, opened on 23 November 1880, was called Eaton Road in honour of the former generous landowner.

COVENTRY CITY RUGBY FOOTBALL TEAM in classic sporting dress photographed in 1891. Many members of this team came from well-to-do families in Coundon and Keresley and also played for the Singer football team (later Coventry City FC) and Warwickshire cricket teams.

COVENTRY CITY FOOTBALL TEAM in the 1927/8 season. The team was originally established by cycle and motor car magnate, George Singer of Coundon Court as a works team in 1883. In 1889 they changed to Coventry City FC, reaching the FA Cup quarter-finals in 1910 and joining the footbal league in 1919.

ACKNOWLEDGEMENTS

I would like to thank Coventry City Libraries Local Studies Section, Central Library and Andrew Mealey (local studies librarian) for allowing me to use the Coventry and Warwickshire collection of photographs as a basis for this book.

My thanks also go to the *Coventry Evening Telegraph* for the use of a number of photographs from their collection.

The remaining photographs are part of my own small collection which refuses to grow despite my continuing quest for old views of the city.

I would also like to thank all those people in the past and present who donate photographs to the city collection, for they have helped make this book possible.

I would like to acknowledge D.A. Norris, M. Tomlinson, R. Sadler, S. Jones, P.W. and L. Thompson, R. Longden, T.S. Pring, B. Male, and H.P. Clayton for the use of photographs still in copyright.